Wildlife Wong
and the
Sumatran Rhino

by
Dr Sarah Pye

Wildlife Wong and the Sumatran Rhino
June 2023

ISBN: 978-0-9806871-9-4 (paperback)
ISBN: 978-0-6451543-9-9 (ebook)

Published by:

estralita
PUBLISHING

Estralita Publishing
ABN: 86 230 144 690
86/7 Grand Parade, Parrearra, QLD, 4575
⊕ www.sarahrpye.com

Sketches: *Woon Bing Chang*
Pencil sketch illustrator: *Woon Bing Chang*
Cover design: *Gram Telen*
Layout design: *Gram Telen*
Wildlife Wong cartoon illustrator: *Isuru Pltawala*
Cover rhino photo: *Dr Wong Siew Te*
Cover author photo: *Amber Grant*

A catalogue record for this
work is available from the
NATIONAL
LIBRARY National Library of Australia
OF AUSTRALIA

Check out what other kids think about this book...

"I think other people should read Wildlife Wong and the Sumatran Rhino so they can learn more about rhinos and sun bears too. I liked it when Wildlife Wong learnt how to stuff animals. It's cool that the Sumatran rhino is a good swimmer like me. I thought the idea of grinding up our toenail clippings and selling them for lots of money was a funny idea, but it shows us how careless we are when we kill rhinos to grind up their horns.

The story was interesting and inspired me to research rhinos more and adopt one. I also thought making a rhino was really cool."

Ava, age 8

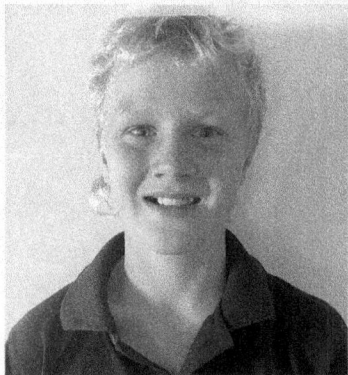

"My favourite part of this book is reading about when William taught Wildlife Wong how to stuff an animal and when Wong stuffed the leopard cat. While reading the book, I felt anger and disbelief, because people have let the rhinos die out.

Wildlife's Wong's work is absolutely amazing. It is great at the end to find out interesting information about the animals I just read about and follow the fun experiments!"

Callan, age 12

"This is a great book (like all of your others... of course) for kids who want to help the environment or just want to read and learn about different animals.

Sumatran rhinos are so interesting. I enjoyed reading all the facts like what they eat, why they are endangered, how we can help, and that their horns are made of a protein called keratin. I never knew Sumatran rhinos descended from Woolly Rhinos.

I love all the stories about Wildlife Wong, especially when Wong tries something new like taxidermy.

The way that you bold and explain difficult words that some kids (including me) might not understand, makes it so much easier and more exciting to read. We are learning so much as we read...... interesting facts, big fancy words and so much more."

Bailey, age 10

Meet Egoo the guard goose

Hi! My name is Sarah, and this is Egoo. She is a model of a bird that I made from wire. I called her Egoo because she looks like a cross between an emu and a goose. Do you like that name?

Near the end of this book, you can learn how to make a model of a Sumatran rhino. I wonder what you will call your rhino?

This is the sixth book I have written about Wildlife Wong. Don't worry if you haven't read the other books because you don't have to read them in order. It includes a story about my friend Wildlife Wong, lots of cool facts, experiments, and interesting ways you can become a scientist.

If you come across a word you don't know, there's a list of new words at the back.

There are videos of the experiments on my website: www.sarahrpye.com. You can also download pages for your own **Nature Journal** and a template for making a unique cover.

Does that sound like fun? I'll remind you again at the end…

Now, let's get on with the story!

A hairy beast

Once upon a time, a VERY long time ago, a gigantic beast roamed freely over much of Earth. It had two horns in a line along its nose. The horn closest to the tip of its nose was long, curved, and pointed. It was used to fight other animals or dig for food. The second horn, which sat between its eyes, was shorter. Can you imagine how heavy its head was? The beast had strong, humped shoulders to hold up its head. It also had stumpy legs, which helped it to balance in a fight.

Could you carry that heavy horn?

Earth was freezing back then and, just like your parents keep canned food in your kitchen pantry for emergencies, the beast stored fat in its hump in case it couldn't find any fresh plants to eat through the bitterly cold winters. It was good at layering its clothes, too. It had two thick, brown fur coats, one on top of the other. The outside layer repelled water like a rain jacket. The **undercoat**, or the fur nearest the skin, kept the beast warm, just like a thick blanket. Sounds toasty, doesn't it?

This amazing beast was called a woolly rhino. It was perfectly adapted to its **frigid** (or freezing) environment.

But Earth's climate and environment are always changing. Little by little, temperatures climbed, and the ice melted. Rivers overflowed, sea levels rose, and some of the land disappeared under water. Volcanos erupted, spewing ash which covered the grassy plains and killed the plants. To top it off, new predators called humans arrived on the scene. They ran fast on two legs and hunted the woolly rhinos with spears.

Woolly rhinos tried to adapt to suit the new world, but they couldn't keep up with all the changes. (It was a bit like a granny who can't get the hang of social media!) Eventually, all the animals died. Woolly rhinos became extinct.

Or did they?

Science detectives make discoveries

Recently, scientists who study **DNA** made a very exciting discovery.

DNA is like the recipe which makes up a species. Scientists **extracted**, or took, DNA from woolly rhino fossils which had been frozen solid in the remaining ice for thousands of years. Then, they took DNA from each of the rhino species on Earth today. They used a computer program to compare the **similarities** and **differences**.

Have you ever used a microscope?

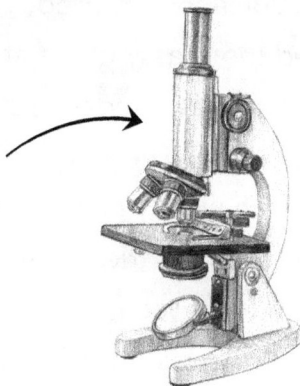

The results surprised them. They discovered that the smallest rhino on Earth was related to the gigantic woolly rhino! Even though we don't have any woolly rhinos anymore, some of the woolly rhino's **genetic** material (another name for DNA) had passed down from one generation to the next for a VERY long time until it became a new species — the Sumatran rhino.

When Wildlife Wong learnt Sumatran rhinos **descended** (or came from) woolly rhinos, he thought they deserved a lot of respect. Wong knew Sumatran rhinos were endangered. They were disappearing fast because people were killing them for their horns. They had survived climate change, floods and **famines**, which made them super **resilient**. But he wondered if this ancient species could survive living on Earth with humans?

Wildlife Wong didn't know it then, but he would be on the frontline of a battle against extinction.

It all started because he loved birds.

What do birds have to do with Sumatran rhinos?

Wildlife Wong is a twitcher. That's not someone who does a crazy type of dance. It's a person who loves to watch birds. Are you a twitcher? Do you like watching bird **antics**, or activities?

If Wildlife Wong wasn't a twitcher, he might never have met a Sumatran rhino called Mina. It's funny how one thing can lead to another, isn't it?

Wong is from a country in Asia called Malaysia, but he travelled to university in another country far away from his home, called Taiwan. Wong studied **veterinary science** and **animal husbandry**.

Basically, that means he learnt how to look after animals.

Wong had a favourite teacher in Taiwan called Kurtis Pei (which sounds like 'pay'). Do you remember reading about Kurtis in **Wildlife Wong and the Orangutan?**

Kurtis ran a wildlife rescue centre on the eastern side of the university campus, and he asked Wong to help clean out the cages and care for the wild animals. This was a dream come true for Wong, so he said yes! Wong loved looking after Polly, the rescued orangutan, and the naughty monkeys or **macaques** (it sounds like 'ma-kaks'). He even loved feeding the tortoise someone abandoned on the doorstep one day in a cardboard box!

Wong loved cuddles with Polly.

PHOTOGRAPH: © WONG SIEW TE

Kurtis thought Wong was a very good worker, so he asked Wong if he would help him do some research. Kurtis told him they could learn all kinds of things by studying animal **scats** (or poo), **stalking** (or following) wild animals, and even by **dissecting** (or cutting up) dead creatures.

It felt like the best present ever when Kurtis gave Wong keys to the vast **laboratory**. (That's a place where scientists work.) Wong wandered around in awe, running his hands over the stainless-steel benches, and peering through a microscope lens at the glass plates below. He opened the freezer and pulled out an **opaque** (not quite see-through) plastic bag about the size of a kitten. The label read: 'Formosan hairy-footed flying squirrel'. The cold bag crinkled as Wong turned it around in his hands, and he caught his frosty breath when two eyes stared at him through the misty plastic.

Wong found he loved working with both live and dead animals. Being busy made him less homesick. But Wong longed for more human company. "Why don't you join the student bird club?" Kurtis suggested. "It's a great way to make friends."

Wong ready for a day of birdwatching.

PHOTOGRAPH: © WONG SIEW TE

Wong took Kurtis's advice one Friday morning. The bird club was going on a weekend twitching adventure to Kenting National Park. He pulled on his T-shirt, slid his arms into his vest-with-many-pockets, and slung his overnight bag across his shoulder. In it were his toothbrush, a change of clothing, a raincoat, gloves, his boots, a notebook and his treasured binoculars. Then he jammed his lucky camouflage hat on his head, plucked up his courage, and rode his bicycle to campus. He locked his bike to the bike rack and walked over to a group of about fifteen students gathered near the motorbike parking. Wong felt **apprehensive**, or nervous, until he noticed some of them were wearing camouflage gear too, and one girl had binoculars around her neck. It made him feel like he would fit in, so he strode forward and said hello!

"Who needs a ride?" said an older boy, and Wong raised his hand. "Hi, my name's William, jump on!" Wong slung his leg over the motorbike bench seat behind William, with his bag squashed between them, and they took off in a **convoy**, or a long line. It was the beginning of many new adventures.

One of them involved dead birds.

Get stuffed!

William liked stuffing birds and I don't mean putting breadcrumbs inside a chicken before you roast it! He liked to take dead birds and make them look like they were alive. William said it was like giving the bird a *new* life and it was called **taxidermy**. Wong was fascinated. He thought about the Formosan hairy-footed flying squirrel which was still in Kurtis's freezer. If William taught him how to be a **taxidermist**, maybe he could stuff that too?

19

One day, William agreed to demonstrate his hobby to the bird club, so Wong and the other twitchers gathered round the table in excited anticipation. A medium size black and white bird, called a treepie, lay in front of them on an **absorbent** sheet, which would soak up liquid. The bird had a strong, black beak and a very long tail. Its legs were pointing up to the ceiling, with its white breast feathers exposed.

William lined his tools up neatly to the left of the bird: a pair of plastic gloves, a **scalpel** (or sharp surgical knife), a **calliper** (or measuring device), tweezers, a shaker of talcum powder, a roll of wire and a **wad** (or bundle) of cotton wool. On the right side of the bird lay a typed checklist. "Can you help write down the measurements, Wong?" William asked, handing over the paper and a pen.

As William worked, the chatter stopped. He pulled on his thin, blue surgical gloves and snapped them into place. Then he cupped the bird in his left palm and measured the length and width of its head with the calliper. William called out the measurements and Wong scribbled them onto the checklist. "When the skin is off, it's floppy," William said. "The measurements help me make the bird look the same when it's stuffed."

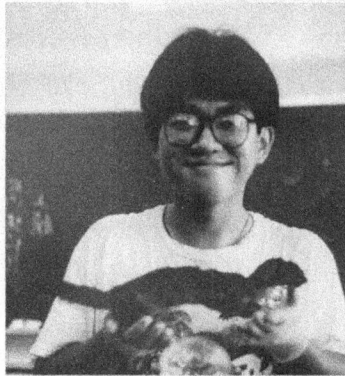

Stuffing animals was really fun!

PHOTOGRAPH: © WONG SIEW TE

William reached for his scalpel. He held the bird firmly with the thumb and forefinger on his left hand, and gently inserted the knife close to its throat. "Don't go too deep," he instructed, "because you want to remove the rib cage in one piece." He folded back the bird's skin and feathers, exposing the insides. "Now we have to peel the skin back really carefully," he said. He grabbed the talcum powder and shook it just like he was putting icing sugar on pancakes. "Talcum powder helps dry the skin, so it's not too slippery!" he said.

Wong watched in awe as William gently pulled the bird's skin inside out. Soon, he had most of the naked body in one hand, and the skin and feathers in the other. Two snips at either end of the spine with the scissors and the skin flopped onto the bench. It looked like an inside-out fluffy sock! The first part of the process was done.

The rest of the afternoon passed quickly as Wong learnt the second and third steps. He couldn't wait to try this out for himself.

Wong's turn

Back in Kurtis's lab, Wong pulled the Formosan hairy-footed flying squirrel from the freezer. While it thawed, he gathered all his equipment and lined it up on the steel bench, just like William had done. Then he skinned the squirrel. When the animal lay naked, and the scraped skin was in his hand, he read his notes for part two.

Wong sprinkled the skin with Borax **granules** until it looked like it was covered in salt. This would **preserve** it, (or protect it from rotting). Then, he took measurements of the body and skull so he could make a wire **mannequin**, (which sounds like 'man-i-kin' and means a model).

22

He cut three pieces of wire and braided them together. Then he did the same again, and again until he had six thick braids of wire. Next, Wong bent the wire braids together to make a stick-figure animal. The first three pieces became the front legs and the head. The next three became the back legs and the tail.

Wong pulled his gloves off and looked at his creation. He was pleased with his work, but it was time to go back to his dorm. The skin would stay covered in the Borax powder overnight before Wong could do part three.

That was the first animal Wong stuffed, but it wasn't the last!

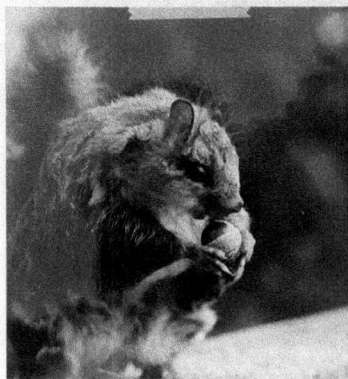

Do you think the stuffed squirrel looks alive?

PHOTOGRAPH: © WONG SIEW TE

Wong goes back home

Wong handed Kurtis his prized stuffed squirrel for safekeeping and wandered around the cages, saying goodbye to all his animal friends. He was happy and sad in equal measure. He knew he would miss his teacher Kurtis and the rescue centre, but he was excited because he had accepted a job at the Malaysian Nature Society, back in his home country. The Malaysian Nature Society wanted the government to protect a wild area in the northern part of Peninsular Malaysia, and they needed to prove why it was important. Wong was paid to **survey**, (or count and **estimate**), animal and plant species.

Wong strung his hammock and tarp between two trees along a riverbank. The sun had dipped below the horizon, so he pulled his hurricane lantern, camp stove, and topographic map from his bag. While he boiled water for instant noodles, Wong decided which way he would explore in the morning.

A safe place for the night!

Wong was woken by the birds' dawn chorus, and he could hear a gibbon booming in the distance. He was eager to get going, so he packed his bag and pulled on his boots. Not far from his camp, Wong came upon a group of broken **saplings** (or young trees). He got closer to look. The break wasn't sharp, like a knife cut, but twisted. There was only one type of animal that broke twigs like that... Wong's heart raced. He searched for more evidence. Not far away, he found telltale scats. Wong was ecstatic! This area was home to the Sumatran rhino!

Wong spent two months surveying the area, but he never actually saw an **elusive** (or shy) rhino. The good news is, his report was so helpful, the Royal Belum State Park became protected.

Finding rhinos is not easy!

PHOTOGRAPH: © WONG SIEW TE

One day, when he was in the office writing his report, the phone rang. It was a **veterinarian**, or animal doctor, from Zoo Malaka. "I'm glad I caught you," said the Indian voice on the other end. "One of our leopard cats has died. Will you come and teach me how to stuff her?"

"If you come, I can introduce you to Mina the Sumatran rhino!"

Wong's first rhino

As Wong steered his motorcycle into the parking lot at Zoo Malaka, he was excited to meet his first rhino. But first there was work to do.

The vet led him to the operating room. The defrosted leopard cat lay on the table. It was about the size of a house cat with big beady eyes for seeing at night, and **mottled** (or spotted) fur just like a leopard. Wong ran his fingers through its soft coat. Then, just as William had taught Wong, he demonstrated the first two steps. The vet wanted to use the cat's real skull, so they **meticulously** (which means very carefully) removed the brain with cotton buds and left the skull soaking in a cleaning solution overnight.

The next morning, they eased the mannequin's back legs into the fur and used tweezers to fill the spaces with small pieces of cotton wool. Then they wrapped cotton around the mannequin's **torso** (the middle of the body) until it matched their measurements. Slowly, Wong turned the skin right side out over the torso and fed the front legs into their fur socks. Next, Wong attached the dried skull to the mannequin, and stretched the skin to cover it. He had two false cats' eyes and a cat's nose, which slotted into their sockets.

Leopard cats look a little like house cats...

After they jammed cotton into all the spaces, Wong taught the vet to sew the skin together with tiny stitches that wouldn't show. They mounted the cat on a **plinth**, or stand, and stood back to admire it with pride. "Thanks so much, Wong," said the vet. "Now, would you like to meet Mina the Sumatran rhino?"

Meeting Mina

Wong watched Mina with wonder and sadness. That morning, he had seen an article in the newspaper which said the police had **confiscated** (or taken away) twelve Sumatran rhino horns from a man in Taiwan. The horns had been illegally poached in Malaysia.

In 1984, a scientist called Nico Van Strein estimated there were somewhere between 481 and 873 Sumatran rhinos left in the wild. But Wong knew that in 1992 there were only seven rhinos in Tabin Wildlife Reserve and twenty-three in Danum Valley Conservation area. With another twelve gone, he did the maths in his head. Can you do it too? How many rhinos were left?

He wondered how so many rhinos had gone in ten years.

Was this rhino one of the last on earth?

PHOTOGRAPH: © WONG SIEW TE

Wong wished the government had tried to stop poaching, or protected the rhino's home, but instead they had created the Asian Rhino Group to solve the problem. The people in the group decided to capture wild rhinos and start a breeding program. Unfortunately, the first few captured rhinos died in the traps, so they changed the traps. Then, the keepers fed the captive rhinos food that African rhinos eat, rather than the leaves and branches they were used to. Some of the rhinos got sick and died. One day, a calf called Erong was caught, and his keepers fed him cow's milk which he couldn't digest. Erong died too.

When Mina's mum was trapped, she was already pregnant. At that time, Mina was the only rhino born in captivity who lived.

Mina and her mum.

Wong stared at her in her lonely pen. Her toenails looked like an elephant's and the skin around her face was wrinkled. Mina's ears twitched to shake off the flies. She turned her head to look directly at him and sang at him as if she was asking for help. Humans had made a lot of mistakes when it came to saving rhinos. So far, Mina had survived, but would her *species* be as lucky?

Another decade goes by

Ten more years passed before Wong **encountered** another rhino. By then, things with the species were **dire** (or really bad).

It was 1999, and Wong was living in the research centre in Danum Valley. He was trapping and tracking sun bears. Just like rhinos, sun bears were in danger from poachers, and he was doing his best to save them. He trapped six bears and put tracking collars around their necks so he could follow them through the jungle and learn about their lives.

Sometimes when he was on a bear hunt, Wong found poachers' **snares** in the forest. A snare is a wire loop tied to a tree. When a sun bear, or a rhino, steps into the loop, it tightens around their leg, and they can't escape. When he found a snare, Wong cut it into tiny pieces with his wire cutter, so it couldn't hurt wildlife anymore. But Wong wasn't always in the rainforest. He also spent time in his office typing up his notes.

One day, before he started typing, Wong checked his email. He opened a message from an organisation called the World Wildlife Fund and a picture of a three-legged Sumatran rhino popped up on his screen. Her name was Puntung.

Poor Puntung had lost her leg in a poacher's snare in Tabin Wildlife Reserve, but she had been saved before the poachers returned to kill her. Wildlife Wong was **livid** (or very angry). He wanted to get in his truck, go to Tabin, find all the snares and rip them out of the rainforest but he was torn: He had important work to do here too. Then, his phone rang. It was someone from the government asking Wong to conduct another rhino survey deep within Danum Valley Conservation Area. This time he wouldn't be alone. There would be ten teams. They would spread out in the jungle to try to find out if there were any wild rhinos left. Wong agreed.

This time Wong had a team to help.

PHOTOGRAPH: © WONG SIEW TE

The first team left the field centre on foot. They carried huge backpacks which weighed 30kg each. Do you know how much YOU weigh? It might be about the same as carrying YOU! They had camping gear, a first aid kit, clothes, enough food for a week, and a map. They had compasses around their neck and a machete in a **sheath** (or covering) tied to their belt. The long,

33

curved knife would help cut a path through the dense rainforest.

Wong waved goodbye to his friends as they crossed the suspension bridge and disappeared into the jungle. The first team trudged through the undergrowth for six days and camped under the sky each night. Eventually, they reached the right spot on their map. Then, they cut down foliage until they had a circle big enough to land a helicopter and called on the radio to say they were ready.

It was Wildlife Wong's turn. He passed his bag up to his assistant in the helicopter and climbed in. Wong was excited and nervous. He had never been in a helicopter before. He clipped the seatbelt and reached for the huge earphones so he could hear the pilot's tinny voice. "Ready for takeoff!" the pilot said, and the helicopter **levitated** straight up. The waving people below got smaller and the trees surrounding the field centre looked like broccoli! Then Wong's stomach lurched into his throat as the helicopter turned and banked towards the east.

Just as he had done for the last survey, Wong found a campsite alongside a river. They needed to be close to water for cleaning and drinking. He expected his team would be in the jungle for about ten days, but they would only stay in this place for three. Wildlife Wong warned the others not to sling their hammocks too close to the bank because of crocodiles. Then he picked two sturdy trees for himself and secured his own bed. Wong used a tarp as a roof and strung a net under the tarp to keep out mosquitoes.

It was time for a good night's sleep!

PHOTOGRAPH: © WONG SIEW TE

Then they all worked together to stretch a bigger tarp across a horizontal branch, creating a roof for their kitchen. The sun was dropping

35

rapidly, and the ear-piercing sound of cicadas rose and fell through the valley. They gathered logs to use as chairs, set up the stove, and started cooking dinner.

What sort of food do you think you would take for ten days in the jungle? It had to be food that wouldn't spoil in the heat because they didn't have a fridge. Wong's team had brought rice, canned curry, anchovies (canned fish), dried meat, spicey sambal sauce, and heaps of instant noodles. Two people brought fishing rods, and Wong hoped they might share what they caught!

In the morning, Wong put on dry socks and laced his hiking boots. He knew it was really important to take care of your feet when you were exploring all day. Some of the others had shoes called Adidas Kampungs. These cheap, rubbery, trainers were perfect for jungle trekking because they had a good strong **tread** (or grip).

As they headed off, it started raining and their shoes stuck in the mud. Wong found a leech on his arm, so he rolled it between his fingers and flicked it away. When they crossed an animal track, they stopped and searched for rhino footprints or scats. Everyone was silent as they listened for rhino songs, but they heard nothing.

They got further from camp, and the jungle thickened. As they pushed through leaves, water soaked through their clothes to their skin. The person in the front got out his parang, or machete. He slashed back and forward in a rhythm, cutting the leaves and making a path. Then his hand slipped on the wet knife handle and the blade sliced into his **shin** (or the bottom part of his leg). He yelled out in pain.

The parang blade was really sharp!

Wong rushed to the front, sat his assistant on a log, opened his backpack and reached for his first aid kit. He unwrapped a **sterile gauze** (which is a clean square of fabric) and put it on the gash. "Hold it firmly with your hand," he instructed the injured man, then he wound a bandage around his friend's leg from his ankle to his knee. "Let's get you back to camp," Wong said. He put his friend's arm around his own shoulders and acted as a crutch. It was very slow going, and they were all exhausted when they reached camp.

For the rest of the week, the injured team member stayed behind and kept their food safe from wild animals. Wong was worried about his cut. He treated it with **antibiotic** cream every evening to make sure it didn't get infected. There were some really nasty diseases in the jungle.

As they stumbled back into camp at the end of the next day, Wong could smell fish frying. He was exhausted, soaked, and he could feel a leech squirming in his boot. Fresh-caught fish and stir-fried wild ferns were just what he needed. They hadn't found anything interesting all day but, when he had a belly full of food, he felt more hopeful. Maybe they would find rhinos tomorrow.

Everything seems better with food...

PHOTOGRAPH: © WONG SIEW TE

Wong unwound his friend's bandage and re-dressed it. Then he took off his wet gear, put paw paw ointment on his own scratches, and Band-Aids on his leech bites. Finally, he crawled into his hammock. Within minutes, he was asleep.

At the end of the 10-day survey, the ten teams had found evidence of only thirteen rhinos in the whole of Danum. Do you remember how many rhinos there were in Danum in 1992? Wong went back to the field centre to keep studying sun bears, but he wondered if rhinos would eventually become extinct.

Every rhino is precious

Wong trapped bears in a barrel trap, which is much kinder than a snare. Before he released them, he used a dart gun to inject the bears with a drug called **anaesthetic** to make them go to sleep. When they stopped moving, he lifted them out of the trap, measured them, weighed them, put a satellite collar around their necks, and left them to wake up alone. After that, he could track them through the rainforest.

Wong measuring a sleeping bear!

PHOTOGRAPH: © WONG SIEW TE

But Wong had run out of anaesthetic drugs, so he called the vet at a place called Sepilok Orangutan Rehabilitation Centre, who looked after the captured rhinos and rescued orangutans. "Yes," they said, "we can give you some", so Wong jumped in his truck and drove for four hours to the vet's office. He was tired when he arrived, and he decided to stay the night.

Before he tucked himself into bed, he wandered over to the rhino enclosure.

There were only two rhinos left in the enclosure now, called Tanjung and Gelugob. Wong leaned on the railing to say hello. He wondered what it would feel like to know you were some of the last of your species? It would be much worse than the homesickness he felt in Taiwan, and he hoped Tanjung and Gelugob had no idea how special they were.

The next morning, Wong woke early. He wanted to get back on the road, so he strolled over to the vet's office to pick up his package. He could hear a family of macaques arguing in a nearby tree with high-pitched screams.

Then another scream pierced the air and ranger James ran towards him from the rhino paddock. "Tanjung is dead!, Tanjung is dead!" he yelled. Chaos broke out. All the staff came out of their offices and ran towards the paddock. Wong followed closely behind. When he reached the enclosure, Wong saw Tanjung pinned to the ground by a huge branch. He looked up to see where it had come from. A tree limb had broken in two and the remaining splinters looked like daggers.

Poor Tanjung didn't make it.

PHOTOGRAPH: © WONG SIEW TE

Wong joined the others inside the pen and together they heaved the murder weapon away.

Tanjung wasn't breathing. His spinal cord, which went from his brain all the way to his bottom, was completely **severed**, or cut in two. "At least he would have died quickly," Wong thought. He could hear Gelugob pacing back and forth in the pen next door and crying out for her friend.

Soon after, lonely Gelugob was moved to a zoo, and the rhino enclosure was abandoned.

But not forever.

The ghosts of rhinos past

Altogether, Wong spent six years trapping and tracking sun bears. That's a really long time, isn't it? By the time he was done, he knew more about sun bears than any other Malaysian. He knew enough to make him worried. Just like rhinos, poachers killed sun bears and, just like rhinos, there were very few sun bears left. When poachers killed adult bears, they sometimes sold the baby sun bears, or cubs, as pets. This was illegal and, if they were caught, the government confiscated the cubs just like the government in Taiwan had confiscated Polly the orangutan.

Wong wondered if he could create a rescue centre for sun bears, like the one Kurtis had made in Taiwan. Perhaps, if he built it in a rainforest, bears would be safe, but they would also be able to dig and climb like they did in the wild.

Wong shared his dream with a young, enthusiastic **architect** from a country called Scotland. An architect is a person who designs buildings. His name was Ian, and he was working at the field centre. Together they sketched ideas and tried to solve all the problems they could think of. How would they fence the rainforest to ensure the animals didn't escape? Would the fence have to be electric? What size buildings did they need? How many pens should they build? Slowly, an image of the centre came together in their heads. Ian drew it up on paper, and Wong's friend Cynthia wrote a **proposal**, which is a suggested plan, to give to the government. They hoped the government would give them money to start building.

Eventually, the answer came back. They could build the rescue centre on the site of the old rhino enclosures.

Ian planning where to build.

PHOTOGRAPH: © WONG SIEW TE

Wong and Ian laced up their boots and trudged through the forest. They stepped over missing planks along the abandoned ironwood walkway, following the **perimeter** (or outside) fence. They climbed the rickety steps and slashed through the overgrown plants to reach the old rhino feeding deck. Both Ian and Wong sat down and looked up at the tall trees reaching for the sky. It felt like the ghosts of rhinos were close. It was a sad place. Wong spoke to the forest,

"I know you have lost a valuable species here," he said, "but perhaps, if we work together, we can save another."

Slowly, the Bornean Sun Bear Conservation Centre grew from the mud until Ian and Wong's dreams came true. The first rescued bears moved into their new home and more followed.

Since those humble beginnings, Wildlife Wong and his team have rescued sixty-five sun bears. Some of them, (like Damai who you can read about in *Wildlife Wong and the Sun Bear*), grew so good at being wild that Wong released them back into Tabin Wildlife Reserve.

Lin May, Thye Lim, Shyamala and Wong planning the new cub school.

PHOTOGRAPH: © WONG SIEW TE

Wong's *new* dream was to build a sun bear cub school in Tabin, where young bears graduated from captivity to freedom. Wong and his assistant, Thye Lim, (which sounds like 'tie-lim'), stepped over liliana vines in their black gumboots, just like he and Ian had done so many years before. This time, they were planning where to put the new cub school. He hoped the new cub school would break the silence left by the rhinos and replace it with barking bears! As he measured the distance between trees, Wong wondered how Damai was doing, and how far away she was from where they were standing.

When their measuring was done, Wong and Thye Lim stopped at Tabin Wildlife Sanctuary to pay their respects to the ancient Sumatran rhinos. Puntung stood on her three legs, unmoving, in a display case. After she died, she had been stuffed, just like Wong's Formosan hairy-footed flying squirrel. She was an important reminder that her species once roamed the jungles of Malaysia. As Wong stared into her unseeing eyes, he vowed he would do everything in his power to make sure sun bears didn't disappear too.

Puntung is still educating people.

Would you like to learn a bit more about rhinos? After that, it's your turn to become a scientist and conduct experiments!

The oldest mammal on earth

All rhinos give birth to live babies and feed them milk. Do you remember what type of animals this makes them? Yes, that's right, they are **mammals**. Sumatran rhinos have lived on Earth longer than any other rhino. In fact, they have lived on Earth longer than any other mammal!

How many types of rhinos are there?

There are five different rhinos in the world. The two species in Africa are called the black rhino and the white rhino. The weirdest thing is they aren't black or white. They are both grey. So why are they called black and white rhinos? It's all about their lips.

The black rhino's top lip is pointed, and the white rhino's lips are wide and square. It is thought the white rhino got its name because there's a language in South Africa called Afrikaans, and the word for wide in Afrikaans is 'wyd' which sounds a bit like 'white'.

There are three types of rhinos in Asia. The greater one-horned rhino lives in India and Nepal. The Javan rhino is only found on the island of Java, and the Sumatran rhino lives in Sumatra and Borneo.

Can you tell which one is a
Sumatran rhino?

How do you tell a Sumatran rhino apart from the other rhinos?

Sumatran rhinos are much smaller than their **predecessors** (or ancestors) the woolly rhinos. They still have hair covering their body, but it's the **equivalent** (or similar to) of wearing a hoodie rather than two fur coats. Their horns are much easier to carry around because they are stumpy, like their legs! They are also much smaller than all the other rhinos. Sumatran rhinos are about 1 metre high, and they weigh an average of about 600kg when they are adults. That's about the same as a cow. White rhinos in Africa can be twice as tall and twice as heavy! Another weird thing is Sumatran rhinos are really excellent swimmers, but the rhinos in Africa aren't!

What do rhinos sound like?

Rhinos make weird and wonderful noises. African rhinos growl and make trumpet calls like elephants when they are fighting. Black rhinos snort when they are angry, sneeze when they are calling out an alarm to other rhinos, and scream if they are scared. When they are relaxed, they make a sound like 'mmwonk'. Can you make that sound?

Sumatran rhinos are sometimes called the 'singing rhino' because they make a squeaky, piercing sound when they want attention, which sounds like singing. If you are able to go on YouTube, you can find a video and listen to their singing...

What do rhinos eat?

All rhinos are **herbivores**, which means they eat plants, not meat. Rhinos are one of the few remaining **megaherbivores** which means they are big plant-eaters. The different species of rhinos live in very different habitats, so they eat different types of plants. Black rhinos use their pointed lips to plug leaves and fruit from trees. White rhinos walk with their square lips close to the ground and graze on (or eat) different types of grasses. Sumatran rhinos chew on leaves, twist shrubs and chomp on mangos and figs.

Yummy leaves!

PHOTOGRAPH: © WONG SIEW TE

Are rhinos endangered?

Three of the five rhino species are critically endangered: black rhinos, Javan rhinos, and Sumatran rhinos. That means there is a high chance they will become extinct. In 2015, since I met my friend Wong, the wild Sumatran rhino was **declared** extinct in Malaysia. In 2019, the last Malaysian captive rhino, called Iman, died too. But there are still about 80 wild rhinos in Indonesia. That means we can still save the species if we act quickly!

The first step is stopping people from killing rhinos.

Why do people kill rhinos?

People kill rhinos for three main reasons. The first is because they are hungry and need something to eat. The second is because they like having a rhino head as a trophy on their wall. This type of slaughter (or killing) happens more in Africa than in Asia and it is mostly done by people from Western countries like the United States or the United Kingdom who have heaps of money and think it is exciting to hunt wild animals as a sport. In some places, this type of hunting is legal. The third reason for killing a rhino is because rhino horns are worth a lot of money.

Rhino horns are made of something called **keratin.** It's a type of protein and it's the same thing that makes up your hair and fingernails. Just like your fingernails, rhino horns keep growing. For over 3,000 years, people in China have believed that powdered rhino horn is a powerful medicine, and they will pay a lot of money for it. Sounds weird, doesn't it? I think they should just chew their fingernails… or maybe we should all collect our toenail clippings, grind them up and sell them for lots of money!

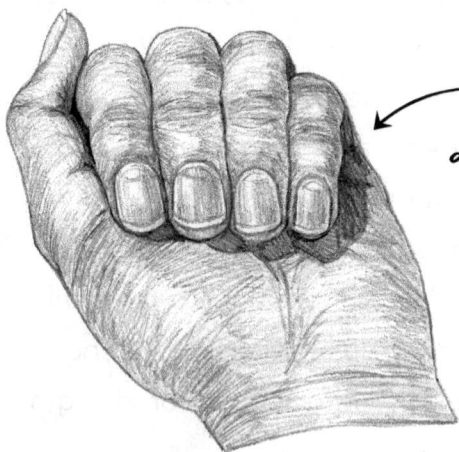

Fingernails and rhino horns are both made of keratin.

How can we save rhinos?

Dedicated people CAN save a species from extinction because it has been done before. Another ancient animal called a bison, (which was also around when woolly rhinos were alive) nearly went extinct. There are now over 2,000 bison! That means there is hope!

Do you remember that the Malaysian government tried to trap rhinos and breed them in captivity? They weren't successful, but the Indonesian government is trying the same thing again. Let's hope they learnt from previous mistakes.

In a country called South Africa, 7,000 rhinos have been killed for their horns, so the people who look after some **reserves**, (or protected areas), have taken a drastic step: they dart the rhinos and, when they are asleep, they saw off their horns, so poachers and trophy hunters won't want to kill them. If some rhinos have horns and others don't, it makes rhino fights a little unfair, but this crazy idea has saved hundreds of rhinos.

Is cutting off horns a good solution?

One important solution is to stop poaching. In some areas, rangers patrol rhino habitat and take away any snares they find. **Trafficking** (or sending rhino horns to other countries) is illegal so, if poachers get caught, they go to jail.

Of course, the best solution would be if people didn't want rhino horns anymore. Scientists have created synthetic (which means 'not natural') medicines which work better than rhino horns. This means everyone can certainly live without rhino horn medicine. That means it is important to educate people.

You can help!

You can help educate your friends by lending them this book. Perhaps you can also do a project on Sumatran rhinos at school to teach even more people?

Instead of asking for a new video game or a bike for your next birthday, why don't you ask your parents to help save Ratu instead? Ratu is the only captive Sumatran rhino in Indonesia who has given birth, and she's done it twice! Her babies are called Andatu and Delilah. Ratu and her calves live at the Sumatran Rhino Sanctuary and if you support the sanctuary, you are helping save the species from extinction. Check it out at: https://www.savetherhino.org/programmes/the-sumatran-rhino-sanctuary/

Experiments
(See videos at sarahrpye.com)

Experiment 1:
Make a rhino mannequin

Do you remember what step two was when stuffing an animal? Yes, that's right, it was making a mannequin in the shape of the animal. And do you remember that Pentung the rhino was stuffed and put on display at Tabin Wildlife Reserve?

We aren't going to stuff a real dead animal today, but we can make a model of a Sumatran rhino!

You will need:

A recycled plastic jar or bottle

A small paper cup

3 toilet rolls

A hot glue gun and glue (with a parent to help!)

Paint

Paint brushes

Two buttons for eyes (optional)

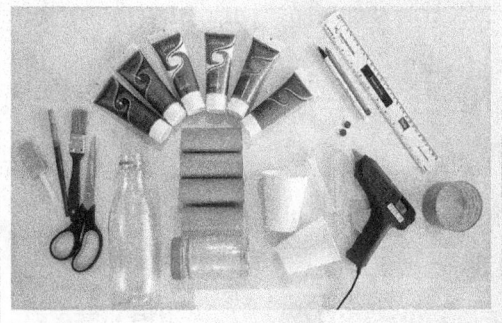

Steps:

Making the legs, tail and horn

1. Take two toilet rolls. Cut one quarter off the length of each toilet roll and then cut the toilet rolls in half lengthways. These will be used to make four legs.

2. On each leg, make 3-5cm long cuts all the way around the top and fan out the top so the legs look a little like a tree with branches. You have now created tabs.

3. Cut the last toilet roll lengthways and roll it out flat. This will be used to cut out a horn and a tail.

4. Measure a triangle on the flat toilet roll where the sides are about 4-5cm long and cut it out. Then cut a strip of the flat toilet roll to make a tail. Don't forget, a rhino's tail almost touches the ground so make it long… you can always trim it later!

5. Lastly, cut out two leaf shapes for ears. Make a small **incision**, or cut, at the base and fold them over to make a cup shape.

Making the head

1. The paper cup will become your rhino head, but it needs a horn so cut a small slit in the side of the paper cup where a horn would be with scissors or a craft knife (and ask an adult for help).

2. Push the triangle through the slit from the inside to the outside.

3. Bend over the part of the triangle which is still inside the cup and glue it in place.

Assembling your rhino

1. Now put the head (the paper cup) onto the body (the plastic jar or bottle) and glue them together using the glue gun. You may have to trim the bottle if it doesn't fit.
2. Put the legs in place. You might have to make some of the slits in the toilet roll legs longer to make them fit better.
3. Secure the legs by putting hot glue on the tabs of the toilet roll legs and attach them to the body. Hold them in place until the glue cools.
4. If your rhino doesn't stand up, trim the legs so it stands properly.
5. Glue your tail onto the rhino's bottom and your ears onto the head.

Painting your rhino

1. Mix your paint colours. Remember, African rhinos are grey, but Sumatran rhinos are a grey-brown colour.

2. Paint your entire rhino. Sumatran rhinos are furry, so don't worry if your brush strokes show...it will look like hairs!

3. If you have buttons, glue them onto your rhino with the hot glue gun when the paint is dry. If you don't have buttons, draw or paint eyes on instead!

You now have a Sumatran rhino!

Experiment 2:
Make Sumatran rhino habitat

Sumatran rhinos won't survive unless we save their habitat. This means we have to stop cutting down trees. Your poor rhino doesn't have a home, so let's make a habitat, or a place for it to live. When you make a model habitat, it is called a **diorama**.

You will need:

A shoebox or cardboard box which is bigger than your rhino mannequin

Paint (green, white, brown, black, yellow and blue are the best colours)

Paint brushes

Paper plates for mixing paint

Green coloured paper

3-4 toilet rolls

Rocks

Small branches which have fallen off trees (we don't want to hurt any trees!)

A hot-glue gun and glue (optional)

Modelling clay (or Blu Tack)

Steps:

1. Stand your cardboard box on its side so the bottom of the box is the backdrop of your habitat, just like a stage.
2. Now paint the back of the rainforest. Start by painting the bottom half with random thicknesses of brown vertical lines that look like tree trunks.
3. Paint the top half with blotches of different greens. It's ok if you overlap the colours.
4. While that backdrop is drying, make your toilet roll trees. If you still have your glue gun from the last experiment, you can use the glue to make textured bark on the toilet roll trees before you paint them. Be careful

though, the glue is hot. Let the glue cool before painting the tree trunks in all kinds of browns, blacks and yellows, then put them aside to dry.

5. Next, paint the floor of the rainforest. You may want a blue stream running through your habitat, and the rest of the floor can be a mixture of brown, grey, green and yellow blotches. Let your diorama dry.

6. When all the paint is dry, cut out leaf shapes from green paper and stick them onto the backdrop with hot glue or Blu Tack. They will stick out a little, which makes the rainforest look three dimensional.

7. Now use real small tree branches to make your tree trunks come alive: Break off pieces and put them inside the toilet roll tree trunks with the leaves standing up. Make sure your finished trees are small enough to fit into your diorama.

8. Place your toilet roll trees on the forest floor of the diorama, leaving enough room for your rhino. Stick them in place with hot glue or modelling clay (Blu Tack).

9. Fix rocks onto the floor of your rainforest in the same way.

10. When your rainforest is finished, it's time for your Sumatran rhino to move in...

Let's stop extinction!

Maybe, one day, you might go to university and learn to be a scientist, just like Wildlife Wong. But why wait?

There are scientists all over the world who are trying to improve what we know about animals. It's a very big job and they need as much help as they can get. When people who aren't scientists (like you) help collect information that scientists need, they are called 'citizen scientists'.

Do you want to be a citizen scientist?

The longest running citizen science project started in the United States on Christmas Day in 1900. It is called the Christmas Bird Count. Can you work out how many years it has been running? There's another bird count you can help with.

Citizen Science Project 1: The Great Backyard Bird Count

Every year in February, people all over the world take time out from school or work, and count birds for another bird project called the Great Backyard Bird Count. This project was the first ever *online* citizen science project which started in 1998.

It doesn't matter if you count one bird, or a hundred, your results help scientists find out where different species of birds live. They can use that information to help protect the birds' habitat. Isn't that amazing? Do you want to take part?

Counting birds can be fun!

This is how you do it:

1. Find out the dates for next February at www. birdcount.org.

2. If you have a smart phone, download the free **Merlin Bird ID** app and install a Bird Pack for the area where you live. It includes a field guide with images and information about birds near you. If you don't have a smart phone, you can download a list of birds in your area at www.ebird.org but if you do this, you also need a bird book.

3. Decide where you want to watch birds. This can be in your backyard or your favourite natural place.

4. Watch birds for at least 15 minutes and record what birds you see. This will be easiest if you have a pair of binoculars, just like Wildlife Wong.

5. If you use the app, when you click 'This is My Bird!', it asks for the name of the location. Maybe you can think up a really cool name like 'Sarah's Secret Sydney Garden' or 'Peter's Paddock in Plymouth'. (Can you tell I like **alliterations**?).

6. If you don't use the app, send your written list to The Great Backyard Bird Count at www.birdcount.org.

7. As soon as you upload or send your data (or information) it is available for scientists to use. You are now a citizen scientist!

Citizen Science Project 2: Project Noah - Signs of Wildlife

Do you remember that Wildlife Wong and his research team found evidence of Sumatran rhinos by searching for scats, twisted trees and footprints? If you look carefully, you can find signs of wildlife where you live too.

Sometimes, I find old nests blown out of trees in a nearby park, or washed-up shells along the beach. Early in the morning, you may come across dew-covered spider webs in the grass or while you are helping your parents, you may find sun-bleached animal bones in the farmyard.

When you find something interesting, take a photo with your camera or phone. Then ask an adult if you can upload it to Project Noah (www.

projectnoah.org) just like other wildlife spotters in 196 countries!

Each task on Project Noah is called a mission, and there are all kinds of amazing missions. The *Signs of Wildlife* mission is a perfect place to upload your photos of bones, webs and shells, but there are heaps of other missions too! For instance, 5,000 people have taken pictures of ladybirds (or ladybugs) and uploaded them to *The Lost Ladybug Project*! This helps scientists find new ladybug species no-one has ever seen before and map where they live.

Can you help scientists map ladybirds?

PHOTOGRAPH: © CREATIVE COMMONS

Be a superhero

Over 42,000 species in the world are close to extinction. That's about one in every three species we know of. That's really sad, isn't it? The list includes 40% of the world's frogs, 37% of sharks, 20% of reptiles and 27% of mammals. That means there are animals where you live that are facing the same fate as the Sumatran rhino.

You can be a superhero and help save an endangered animal, just like Wildlife Wong is helping save sun bears. Where I live, there's a group of people who plant eucalyptus trees (which sounds like *you-ca-lip-tus*) so endangered koalas have a place to live. There's another group of turtle watchers who patrol beaches to make sure endangered loggerhead turtles can get ashore safely and lay their eggs.

Where you live, there may be people who toss wildflower seeds on their lawn and let them grow wild so bees don't become endangered, or there might be a group that scoops out rubbish from the local pond so endangered frogs can **spawn** (or lay their eggs).

Why don't you ask an adult to help you search for the conservation groups in your area, then see if you can spend one Saturday helping them?

New words

Some of the words or phrases in this book are bold. Here's what they mean. They are in alphabetical order. After the word, it tells you what kind of word it is.

A noun (n) is a person, place or thing.

A verb (v) is a doing word.

An adjective (adj) describes (or adds to) a noun.

An adverb (adv) describes (or adds to) a verb.

Once you learn a new word, try using it!

Absorbent (adj) – Something that soaks up liquid

Alliteration (n) – A group of words starting with the same letter or sound

Anaesthetic (n) – A medicine to make an animal or human go to sleep

Animal husbandry (n) – The science of breeding and caring for farm animals

Antibiotic (n) – A medicine that stops germs growing

Antics (n) – Crazy activities or behaviour

Apprehensive (v) – To be nervous

Architect (n) – A person who designs buildings

Calliper (n) – A measuring device

Confiscated (adj) – Taken away or caught

Convoy (n) – A long line of vehicles

Declared (v) – Formally announced something

Descended from (v) – Came from

Differences (n) – The way things are not the same

Diorama (n) – A 3-dimensional model of a scene or habitat

Dire (adj) – Really bad or serious

Dissecting (v) – Cutting up a body or plant to study it

Elusive (adj) – Difficult to find

Encountered (v) – Came across something unexpectedly

Equivalent (adj) – Equal in value or function

Estimate (n) – A calculated guess

Extracted (v) – Took out

Famine (n) – A period of time where there is no food

Frigid (adj) – Really cold

Genetic (adj) – Relating to genes or DNA

Granules (n) – Small particles, (like sugar or sand)

Graze on (v) – To feed on something like grass

Herbivore (n) – An animal that only eats plants

Incision (n) – A cut

Keratin (n) – A protein which makes up hair and fingernails

Laboratory (n) – The room where scientists conduct experiments

Levitated (v) – Rose straight up and hovered in the air

Livid (adj) – Very angry

Macaque (n) – A type of monkey

Mammal (n) – An animal with warm blood and fur that feeds its babies milk

Mannequin (n) – A life-like model

Megaherbivore (n) – A very large animal that only eats plants

Meticulously (adv) – Very carefully

Mottled (adj) – Spotted or splotchy

Opaque (adj) – Transparent, or not see-through

Perimeter (n) – The outside edge, or boundary, of a shape

Plinth (n) – A heavy base or stand

Predecessor (n) – An ancestor or someone that came before

Preserve (v) – To protect something from rotting

Proposal (n) – A suggested plan

Reserve (n) – A protected area

Resilient (adj) – To be able to recover quickly from difficult situations

Saplings (n) – Young trees

Scalpel (n) – A sharp surgical knife

Scats (n) – Animal droppings or poo

Sculpture (n) – A three-dimensional artwork

Severed (adj) – Cut off

Sheath (a) – A knife cover

Shin (n) – The front of a leg, below the knee

Similarities (n) – Features which are the same

Slaughter (v) – To kill lots of animals, sometimes cruelly

Snares (n) – Poacher's wire traps

Stalking (v) – Following quietly

Sterile gauze (n) – A clean square of medical fabric

Survey (v) – To observe and count

Synthetic (adj) – Man-made or not natural

Taxidermist (n) – Someone who does taxidermy

Taxidermy (n) – Stuffing dead animals

Torso (n) – The section of the body without the head, legs or arms

Trafficking (v) – Selling things illegally in different countries

Tread (n) – The bottom of a shoe that grips

Undercoat (n) – The fur nearest the skin

Veterinarian (n) – An animal doctor

Veterinary science (n) – The science of looking after the health of animals

Wad (n) – A tight bundle

Do you want to read more?

Wildlife Wong has adventures with all kinds of animals!

Why not check out these stories next?

Don't forget, you can find videos of the experiments, and download your own **Nature Journal** on my website: www.sarahrpye.com

Let us know what you think!

You can find out more, or contact me and Wildlife Wong using the following links:

Sarah Pye

- FB: https://www.facebook.com/SarahRPye
- Instagram: https://www.instagram.com/author_sarahrpye/
- Twitter: https://twitter.com/AuthorSarahPye
- YouTube: https://www.youtube.com/@sarahrpyeauthorspeakerenvi6784

Wildlife Wong

- Facebook: https://www.facebook.com/wong.s.te.1
- Instagram: https://www.instagram.com/wongsiewte/

Bornean Sun Bear Conservation Centre

- Website: https://www.bsbcc.org.my/
- Facebook: https://www.facebook.com/sunbear.bsbcc
- Instagram: https://www.instagram.com/bsbcc/
- Twitter: https://twitter.com/BSBCC_SunBear
- YouTube: https://www.youtube.com/@BSBCCSUNBEAR

For teachers and parents:

Sarah Pye loves visiting schools and festivals, both in person and online, to teach kids more about the rainforest.

For more information, visit:

🌐 **www.sarahrpye.com**

Do you want Sarah to come to your school?